# DEATH

By Alan Watts
Book IV in the Illustrated Series
THE ESSENCE OF ALAN WATTS

ALAN WATTS " . . . has provided a series of sensitively illustrated jewel-books for the searching spirits of this century . . . . "
—Joseph Campbell

Photographs by Mike Powers and Maria Demarest

CELESTIAL ARTS
Millbrae, California

Copyright©1975 by Celestial Arts
231 Adrian Road, Millbrae, California 94030

No part of this book may be reproduced by any mechanical, photographic, or electronic process, or in the form of a phonographic recording, nor may it be stored in a retrieval system, transmitted, or otherwise copied for public or private use without the written permission of the publisher.

First Printing, January 1975
Made in the United States of America
Cover photo of Alan Watts by Margo Moore

Library of Congress Cataloging in Publication Data

Watts, Alan Wilson, 1915-1973.
   Death.

   (His The essence of Alan Watts ; book 4)
   1. Death. I. Title.
B945.W321 1974, vol. 4 (BD444) 191s (128'.5) 74-25825
ISBN 0-912310-85-5

# THE STORY OF ALAN WATTS

For more than twenty years Alan Watts earned a reputation as the foremost interpreter of Eastern philosophies to the West. Beginning at the age of 20, when he wrote *The Spirit of Zen*, he developed an audience of millions who were enriched by his offerings through books, tape recordings, radio, television, and public lectures.

He wrote 25 books, each building toward a personal philosophy that he shared, in complete candor and joy, with his readers and listeners throughout the world. They presented a model of individuality and self-expression that can be matched by few contemporaries. His life and work reflect an astonishing adventure: he was editor, Anglican priest, graduate dean, broadcaster, and author-lecturer. He had fascinations for cooking, calligraphy, singing, and dancing. He held fellowships from Harvard University and the Bollingen Foundation and was Episcopal Chaplain at Northwestern University. He became professor and dean of the American Academy of Asian Studies in San Francisco, made the television series "Eastern Wisdom and Modern Life" for the National Educational Television, and served as visiting consultant to many psychiatric institutes and hospitals. He traveled widely with students in Japan.

Born in England in 1915, Alan Watts attended King's School Canterbury, served on the Council of the World Congress of Faiths (1936–38), and came to the United States in 1938. He held a Master's Degree in Theology from Seabury-Western Theological Seminary and an Honorary D.D. from the University of Vermont in recognition of his work in Comparative Religion.

Alan Watts died in 1973. *The Essence of Alan Watts*, a series of nine books in the unique *Celestial Arts* format, includes edited transcripts by his wife, Mary Jane Watts, of videotaped lectures that were produced by his friend, Henry Jacobs, and filmed by his son, Mark Watts, in the last years of his life.

I've always been fascinated with the idea of death as far back as I can remember, from earliest childhood. You may think that's kind of morbid, but when a child at night says the phrase *If I should die before I wake,* there's something about it that's absolutely weird. What would it be like to go to sleep and never wake up? Most reasonable people just dismiss the thought. They say, "You can't image that"; they shrug their shoulders and say, "Well, that will be that."

But I'm one of those ornery people who aren't content with an answer like that. Not that I'm trying to find something else beyond that, but I am absolutely fascinated with what it would be like to go to sleep and never wake up. Many people think it would be like going into the dark forever or being buried alive. Obviously it wouldn't be like that at all! Because we know darkness by contrast, and only by contrast, with light.

I have a friend, a girl, who is very intelligent and articulate, who was born blind and hasn't the faintest idea what darkness is. The word means as little to her as the word light. So it is the same for you; you are not aware of darkness when you are asleep.

If you went to sleep, into unconsciousness for always and always, it wouldn't be at all like going into the dark; it wouldn't be at all like being buried alive. As a matter of fact, it would be as if you had never existed at all! Not only you, but everything else as well. You would be in that state, as if you had never been. And, of course, there would be no problems, there would be no one to regret the loss of anything. You couldn't even call it a tragedy because there would be no one to experience it as a tragedy. It would be a simple—nothing at all. Forever and for never. Because, not only would you have no future, you would also have no past and no present.

At this point you are probably thinking, "Let's talk about something else." But I'm not content with that, because this makes me think of two other things. First of all, the state of nothingness makes me think that the only thing in my experience close to nothingness is the way my head looks to my eye. I seem to feel there is a world out there confronting my eye, and then behind my eye there isn't a black spot, there isn't even a hazy spot. There's nothing at all! I'm not aware of my head, as it were, as a black hole in the middle of all this luminous visual experience. It doesn't even have very clear edges. The field of vision is an oval, and behind this oval of vision there is nothing at all. Of course, if I use my fingers and touch I can feel something behind my eyes; if I use the sense of sight alone there is just nothing there at all. Nevertheless, out of that blankness, I see.

The second thing it makes me think of is when I'm dead I am as if I never had been born, and that's the way I was before I was born. Just as I try to go back behind my eyes and find what is there I come to a blank, if I try to remember back and back and back to my earliest memories and behind that—nothing, total blank. But just as I know there's something behind my eyes by using my fingers on my head, so I know through other sources of information that before I was born there was something going on. There were my father and my mother, and their fathers and mothers, and the whole material environment of the Earth and its life out of which they came, and behind that the solar system, and behind that the galaxy, and behind that all the galaxies, and behind that another blank—space. I reason that if I go back when I'm dead to the state where I was before I was born, couldn't I happen again?

What has happened once can very well happen again. If it happened once it's extraordinary, and it's not really very much more extraordinary if it happened all over again. I do know I've seen people die and I've seen people born after them. So after I die not only somebody but myriads of other beings will be born. We all know that; there's no doubt about it. What worries us is that when we're dead there could be nothing at all forever, as if that were something to worry about. Before you were born there was this same nothing at all forever, and yet you happened. If you happened once you can happen again.

Now what does that mean? To look at it in its very simplest way and to properly explain myself, I must invent a new verb. This is the verb *to I*. We'll spell it with the letter *I* but instead of having it as a pronoun we will call it a verb. The universe *I's*. It has *I'd* in me it *I's* in you. Now let's respell the word *eye*. When I talk about *to eye*, it means to look at something, to be aware of something. So we will change the spelling, and will say the universe *I's*. It becomes aware of itself in each one of us, and it keeps the *I'ing*, and everytime it *I's* every one of us in whom it *I's* feels that he is the center of the whole thing. I know that you feel that you are I in just the same way that I feel that I am I. We all have the same background of nothing, we don't remember having done it before, and yet it has been done before again and again and again, not only before in time but all around us everywhere else in space is everybody, is the universe *I'ing*.

Let me try to make this clearer by saying it is the universe *I'ing*. Who is *I'ing*? What do you mean by *I*? There are two things. First, you can mean your ego, your personality. But that's not your real *I'ing*, because your personality is your idea of your self, your image of yourself, and that's made up of how you feel yourself, how you think about yourself thrown in with what all your friends and relations have told you about yourself. So your image of yourself obviously isn't you any more than your photograph is you or any more than the image of *anything* is *it*. All our images of ourselves are nothing more than caricatures. They contain no information for most of us on how we grow our brains, how we work our nerves, how we circulate our blood, how we secrete with our glands, and how we shape our bones. That isn't contained in the sensation of the image we call the ego, so obviously, then the ego image is not my self.

My self contains all these things that the body is doing, the circulation of the blood, the breathing, the electrical activity of the nerves, all this is me but I don't know how it's constructed. And yet, I do all that. It is true to say I breathe, I walk, I think, I am conscious—I don't know how I manage to be, but I do it in the same way as I grow my hair. I must therefore locate the center of me, my *I'ing*, at a deeper level than my ego which is my image or idea of myself. But how deep do we go?

We can say the body is the *I*, but the body comes out of the rest of the universe, comes out of all this energy—so it's the universe that's *I'ing*. The universe *I's* in the same way that a tree apples or that a star shines, and the center of the appling is the tree and the center of the shining is the star, and so the basic center of self of the *I'ing* is the eternal universe or eternal thing that has existed for ten thousand million years and will probably go on for at least that much more. We are not concerned about how long it goes on, but repeatedly it *I's*, so that it seems absolutely reasonable to assume that when I die and this physical body evaporates and the whole memory system with it, then the awareness that I had before will begin all over once again, not in exactly the same way, but that of a baby being born.

Of course, there will be myriads of babies born, not only baby human beings but baby frogs, baby rabbits, baby fruit flies, baby viruses, baby bacteria—and which one of them am I going to be? Only one of them and yet every one of them, this experience comes always in the singular one at a time, but certainly one of them. Actually it doesn't make much difference, because if I were born again as a fruit fly I would think that being a fruit fly was the normal ordinary course of events, and naturally I would think that I was an important person, a highly cultured being, because fruit flies obviously have a high culture. We don't even know how to look at it. But probably they have all sorts of symphonies and music, and artistic performances in the way light is reflected on their wings in different ways, the way they dance in the air, and they say, "Oh, look at her, she has real style, look how the sunlight comes off her wings." They in their world think they are as important and civilized as we do in our world. So, if I were to wake up as a fruit fly I wouldn't feel any different than I do when I wake up as a human being. I would be used to it.

Well, you say, "It wouldn't be me! Because if it were me again I would have to remember how I was before!" Right, but you don't know, remember, how you were before and yet you are content enough to be the me that you are. In fact, it's a thoroughly good arrangement in this world that we don't remember what it was like before. Why? Because variety is the spice of life, and if we remembered, remembered, remembered having done this again and again and again we should get bored. In order to see a figure you have to have a background, in order that a memory be valuable you also have to have a *forgettory*. That's why we sleep every night to refresh ourselves; we go into the unconscious so that coming back to the conscious is again a great experience.

Day after day we remember the days that have gone on before, even though there is the interval of sleep. Finally there comes a time when, if we consider what is to our true liking, we will want to forget everything that went before. Then we can have the extraordinary experience of seeing the world once again through the eyes of a baby—whatever kind of baby. Then it will be completely new and we will have all the startling wonder that a child has, all the vividness of perception which we wouldn't have if we remembered everything forever.

The universe is a system which forgets itself and then again remembers anew so there's always constant change and constant variety in the span of time. It also does it in the span of space by looking at itself through every different living organism, giving an all-around view.

That is a way of getting rid of prejudice, getting rid of a one-sided view. Death in that sense is a tremendous release from monotony. It puts an end to all of total forgetting in a rhythmic process of on/off, on/off so you can begin all over again and never be bored. But the point is that if you can fantasize the idea of being nothing for always and always, what you are really saying is *after I'm dead the universe stops,* and what I'm saying is *it goes on* just as it did when you were born. You may think it incredible that you have more than one life, but isn't it incredible that you have this one? That's astonishing! And it can always happen again and again and again!

What I am saying then is just because you don't know how you manage to be conscious, how you manage to grow and shape your body, doesn't mean that you're not doing it. Equally, if you don't know how the universe shines the stars, constellates the constellations, or galactifies the galaxies—you don't know but that doesn't mean that you aren't doing it just the same way as you are breathing without knowing how you breathe.

If I say really and truly I am this whole universe, or this particular organism is an *I'ing* being done by the whole universe, then somebody could say to me, "Who the hell do you think you are? Are you God? Do you warm up the galaxies? *Canst' thou bind the sweet influences of the Pleiades or loosen the bonds of Orion?*" And I reply, "Who the hell do you think you are! Can you tell me how you grow your brain, how you shape your eyeballs, and how you manage to see? Well, if you can't tell me that, I can't tell you how I warm up the galaxy. Only I've located the center of myself at a deeper and more universal level than we are, in our culture, accustomed to do."

So then, if that universal energy is the real me, the real self which *I's* as different organisms in different spaces or places, and happening again and again at different times, we've got a marvelous system going in which you can be eternally surprised. The universe is really a system which keeps on surprising itself.

Many of us have an ambition, especially in an age of technological competence, to have everything under our control. This is a false ambition because you've only got to think for one moment what it would be like to really know and control everything. Supposing we had a supercolossal technology which could go to our wildest dreams of technological competence so that everything that is going to happen would be foreknown, predicted, and everything would be under our control. Why, it would be like making love to a plastic woman! There would be no surprise in it, no sudden answering touch as when we touch another human being. There comes out a response, something unexpected, and that's what we really want.

You can't experience the feeling you call self unless it's in contrast with the feeling of other. It's like known and unknown, light and dark, positive and negative. Other is necessary in order for you to feel self. Isn't that the arrangement you want? And, in the same way, couldn't you say the arrangement you want is not to remember? Memory is always, remember, a form of control: *I've got it in mind, I know your number, you're under control.* Eventually you want to release that control.

Now if you go on remembering and remembering and remembering, it's like writing on a piece of paper and going on writing and writing until there is no space left on the paper. Your memory is filled up and you need to wipe it clean so you can begin to write on it once more.

That's what death does for us: It wipes the slate clean and also, for looking at it from the point of view of population and the human organism on the planet, it keeps cleaning us out! A technology which would enable each one of us to be immortal would progressively crowd the planet with people having hopelessly crowded memories. They would be like people living in a house where they had accumulated so much property, so many books, so many vases, so many sets of knives and forks, so many tables and chairs, so many newspapers that there wouldn't be any room to move around.

To live we need space, and space is a kind of nothingness, and death is a kind of nothingness—it's all the same principle. And by putting blocks or spaces of nothingness, spaces of *space* in between spaces of *something*, we get life properly spaced out. The German word *lebensraum* means room for living, and that's what space gives us, and that's what death gives us.

Notice that in everything I've said about death I haven't brought in anything that I could call spookery. I haven't brought in any information about anything that you don't already know. I haven't invoked any mysterious knowledge about souls, memory of former lives, anything like that; I've just talked about it in terms that we already know. If you believe the idea that life beyond the grave is just wishful thinking, I'll grant that.

Let's assume that it is wishful thinking and when we are dead there just won't be anything. That'll be the end. Notice, first of all, that's the worst thing you've got to fear. Does it frighten you? Who's going to be afraid? Supposing it ends— no more problems.

But then you will see that this nothingness, if you've followed my argument, is something you'd *bounce* off from again just as you bounced in in the first place when you were born. You bounced out of nothingness. Nothingness is a kind of bounce because it implies that nothing implies something. You bounce back all new, all different, nothing to compare it with before, a refreshing experience.

You get this sense of nothingness, just like you've got the sense of nothing behind your eyes, very powerful frisky nothingness underlying your whole being. There's nothing in that nothing to be afraid of. With that sense you can come on like the rest of your life is gravy because you're already dead: You know you're going to die.

We say the only things certain are death and taxes. And the death of each one of us now is as certain as it would be if we were going to die five minutes from now. So where's your anxiety? Where's your hangup? Regard yourself as dead already so that you have nothing to lose. A Turkish proverb says, "He who sleeps on the floor will not fall out of bed." So in the same way is the person who regards himself as already dead.

Therefore, you are virtually nothing. A hundred years from now you will be a handful of dust, and that will be for real. All right now, act on that reality. And out of that ... nothing. You will suddenly surprise yourself: The more you know you are nothing the more you will amount to something.

## OTHER BOOKS by ALAN WATTS

The Spirit of Zen
The Meaning of Happiness
The Theologia Mystica of St. Dionysius
Behold the Spirit
The Supreme Identity
The Wisdom of Insecurity
Myth and Ritual in Christianity
The Way of Liberation in Zen Buddhism
The Way of Zen
Nature, Man, and Woman
This Is It
Psychotherapy East and West
The Joyous Cosmology
The Two Hands of God
Beyond Theology: The Art of Godmanship
Nonsense
The Book: On the Taboo Against Knowing Who You Are
Does It Matter? Essays on Man's Relation to Materiality
Erotic Spirituality
In My Own Way: An Autobiography
The Art of Contemplation

To order tapes of Alan Watts' lectures, send for a free catalog to:
EU, Box 361, Mill Valley, California 94941

## OTHER BOOKS OF INTEREST FROM
## CELESTIAL ARTS

THE ESSENCE OF ALAN WATTS. The basic philosophy of Alan Watts in nine illustrated volumes. Now available:
GOD. 64 pages, paper, $3.95
MEDITATION. 64 pages, paper, $3.95
NOTHINGNESS. 64 pages, paper, $3.95
TIME. 64 pages, paper, $3.95
NATURE OF MAN. 64 pages, paper, $3.95

WILL I THINK OF YOU. Leonard Nimoy's warm and compelling sequel to You & I. 96 pages, paper, $3.95

THE HUMANNESS OF YOU, Vol. I & Vol. II. Walt Rinder's philosophy rendered in his own words and photographs. Each: 64 pages, paper, $2.95.

MY DEAREST FRIEND. The compassion and sensitivity that marked Walt Rinder's previous works are displayed again in this beautiful new volume. 64 pages, paper, $2.95.

ONLY ONE TODAY. Walt Rinder's widely acclaimed style is again apparent in this beautifully illustrated poem. 64 pages, paper, $2.95

THE HEALING MIND by Dr. Irving Oyle. A noted physician describes what is known about the mysterious ability of the mind to heal the body. 128 pages, cloth, $7.95; paper, $4.95.

I WANT TO BE USED not abused by Ed Branch. How to adapt to the demands of others and gain more pleasure from relationships. 80 pages, paper, $2.95.

INWARD JOURNEY Art and Psychotherapy For You by Margaret Keyes. A therapist demonstrates how anyone can use art as a healing device. 128 pages, paper, $4.95.

PLEASE TRUST ME by James Vaughan. A simple, illustrated book of poetry about the quality too often lacking in our experiences—Trust. 64 pages, paper, $2.95.

LOVE IS AN ATTITUDE. The world-famous book of poetry and photographs by Walter Rinder. 128 pages, cloth, $7.95; paper, $3.95.

THIS TIME CALLED LIFE. Poetry and photography by Walter Rinder. 160 pages, cloth, $7.95; paper, $3.95.

SPECTRUM OF LOVE. Walter Rinder's remarkable love poem with magnificently enhancing drawings by David Mitchell. 64 pages, cloth, $7.95; paper, $2.95.

GROWING TOGETHER. George and Donni Betts' poetry with photographs by Robert Scales. 128 pages, paper, $3.95.

VISIONS OF YOU. Poems by George Betts, with photographs by Robert Scales. 128 pages, paper, $3.95.

MY GIFT TO YOU. New poems by George Betts, with photographs by Robert Scales. 128 pages, paper, $3.95.

YOU & I. Leonard Nimoy, the distinguished actor, blends his poetry and photography into a beautiful love story. 128 pages, cloth, $7.95; paper, $3.95.

I AM. Concepts of awareness in poetic form by Michael Grinder. Illustrated in color by Chantal. 64 pages, paper, $2.95.

GAMES STUDENTS PLAY (And what to do about them.) A study of Transactional Analysis in schools, by Kenneth Ernst. 128 pages, cloth, $7.95; paper, $3.95.

A GUIDE FOR SINGLE PARENTS (Transactional Analysis for People in Crisis.) T.A. for single parents by Kathryn Hallett. 128 pages, cloth, $7.95; paper, $3.95.

THE PASSIONATE MIND (A Manual for Living Creatively with One's Self.) Guidance and understanding from Joel Kramer. 128 pages, paper, $3.95.